Just the Facts

Heroin

Sean Connolly

Heinemann Library
Chicago, Illinois

Designed by M2 Graphic Design
Printed in Hong Kong by South China Printers
Originated by Ambassador Litho Ltd.

05 04 03 02 01
10 9 8 7 6 5 4 3 2

Library of Congress Cataloging-in-Publication Data
Connolly, Sean, 1956-
  Heroin / Sean Connolly.
    p. cm. – (Just the facts)
  Includes bibliographical references and index.
  Summary: Examines the history, nature, sources, and effects of heroin, the dangers of its use, and treatment for addiction to it.
  ISBN 1-57572-257-7 (library)
  1. Heroin habit—Prevention—Juvenile literature. 2. Heroin habit—United States—Prevention—Juvenile literature. 3. Heroin—Juvenile literature. [1. Heroin. 2. Drug abuse.] I. Title. II. Series.

HV5822.H4 C63 2000
362.29'3—dc21

00-025652

Acknowledgments
The Publishers would like to thank the following for permission to reproduce photographs:
Camera Press: pg.24, pg.46; David Hoffman: pg.5, pg.11, pg.51; Frank Spooner: pg.28; Janine Wiedel: pg.23; Magnum Photos: pg.29, pg.45, Wylie Donovan pg.9, Michael Nichols pg.34, pg.35, Griffiths pg.36, Patrick King pg.37, Gilles Press pg.49; Mary Evans Picture Library: pg.18, pg.19; Network: Gideon Mendel pg.17; Photofusion: Nicky Johnson pg.42; Redferns: William Gotlieb pg.22; Rex Features: pg.6, pg.7, pg.11, pg.13, pg.15, pg.21, pg.25, pg.33, pg.40, pg.43, Jon Blum pg.31, Action Press pg.39; Science Photo Library: pg.47; The Stock Market: pg.26, pg.27.

Cover photograph reproduced with permission of M2 Graphic Design.

Every effort has been made to contact copyright holders of any material reproduced in this book.
Any omissions will be rectified in subsequent printings if notice is given to the publisher.

Our special thanks to Pamela G. Richards, M.Ed., for her help in the preparation of the book.

Some words are shown in bold, **like this.** You can find out what they mean by looking in the glossary.

Contents

Introduction

Heroin is a drug of extremes. For many people it is the most feared drug, while for others it is the most dramatic way of escaping the cares and boredom of everyday life. Because heroin is highly addictive, it is the drug that immediately springs to mind when people talk about **dependence** and drug-related crime. Heroin use is a serious problem in the United States, and it forms the backbone of drug treatment programs here and in many other countries.

Escapism with a price

Just why do people take heroin, if it has so many associations with illness and death? The answer can be reduced to one word: escape. Heroin does not promise to lift the spirits or offer users a new psychological perspective. What users experience is a short-lived escape from life while the drug takes effect. Gradually, as people become used to the drug, the sense of comfort that they associate with heroin fades. It is replaced by an intense craving for the drug and then relief when they have found another dose. Eventually, it becomes increasingly difficult to return to the life they had tried to escape from in the first place.

If this sounds depressing, it is. Very few heavy heroin users find any pleasure in the drug. Instead, they come to need more and more of it just to feel "normal."

A familiar story

Heroin abuse is a serious problem in the modern world. The drug is derived from the opium poppy, and people have experimented with different forms of it for more than 4,000 years. Users of the drug were apparently driven by an urge to escape reality. Such urges have been recorded by writers throughout history, from such works as Homer's *Odyssey* to Irvine Welsh's *Trainspotting*, an account of modern Edinburgh 2,700 years later. While the drug produced from the opium poppy has remained the same over the centuries, the means of taking it and the dangers involved have become more complicated.

People who take heroin, a drug derived from the opium poppy, require an assortment of equipment.

What Is Heroin?

Heroin is a member of the group of drugs known as **opiates,** or drugs derived from the opium poppy. Opium is the dried form of a milky substance produced in the poppy. The substance contains codeine and morphine, two very effective painkillers that are used legitimately today. Heroin is morphine with an extra chemical group added to make it more **soluble** in fat. This solubility means that heroin can enter the brain faster than morphine.

Pure heroin, or "white lady," is a white powder. However, by the time people buy it on the street the drug is light brown. From the time the drug is produced to when it is bought on the street, its **purity** has decreased from 100 percent to somewhere between 20 and 60 percent. Pure heroin is often cut, or mixed, with Tylenol™, sugar, or **tranquilizers**, to stretch the original supply and increase the dealer's profit. Heroin use can lead to trouble on many different fronts. Not only does it harm the user and lead to **overdose**, it harms the user's family relationships and society in general.

Because many users mix heroin with other drugs, including alcohol, they increase the risk of life-threatening medical side effects. Many users who **inject** heroin run the additional risk of **HIV** infection or **hepatitis** because they share needles and pass on infection. Heroin is also powerfully **addictive,** both physically and mentally, and it can be extremely hard to break the cycle of **dependence.** Obtaining a steady supply of heroin can cause serious money problems; many desperate users turn to crime to get money for the drug.

"Smack by name, then it literally smacks you in the face."

(A British heroin user and prison inmate)

A heroin user opens a paper "wrap," which contains a single dose of the drug.

Into the cocoon

Once taken, heroin is quickly absorbed into the bloodstream and soon reaches the brain. First-time users report different effects from the drug. Some people feel little or no effect from their first dose, or *hit,* of heroin. Others find the experience immediately unpleasant and feel nauseous. Some people, though, get a warm feeling that starts in the belly and then spreads across the body, seeming to wrap them in a glow of well-being. Many users find this warm, dreamy feeling comforting. Responsibilities seem to drift away, and the user experiences the sensation of "returning to the womb." Other users describe it as being wrapped in a cocoon.

Many of the nicknames for heroin describe the way it looks and feels. While the names "white lady" and "brown" refer to its color at different levels of purity, the name "smack" describes the hard and sudden impact the user feels when the drug is **injected.**

How people take heroin

Heroin, like most **opiates,** dissolves in fatty substances and so can cross through body cells. Therefore, the drug is easily absorbed into the body through many different routes. Heroin can be sniffed (or "snorted"), smoked, or injected. When sniffed, heroin is absorbed into the bloodstream through the nose. When smoked, heroin enters the bloodstream very quickly through the lining of the lungs. Many people who become regular heroin users first smoke the drug.

Eventually, regular users come to need more powerful effects from the drug. They resort to injecting heroin directly into the bloodstream through a vein. Before injecting the drug, a heroin user must dissolve it in a liquid.

Heroin and Addiction

Even people unfamiliar with drugs know that heroin is **addictive.** But what does this mean? And how true are the stories that people can become addicted to heroin after just one session?

Defining the problem

Several medical texts define **addiction** as "the repetitive, compulsive use of a substance that occurs despite negative consequences to the user." However, drug workers prefer to use the word **dependence** rather than addiction. There are two types of dependence: psychological and physical. Certain chemicals in the brain, nicknamed *the pleasure circuits*, are activated by drugs that produce psychological dependency. Heroin is one of those drugs.

Tracing the pleasure circuit

Heroin produces psychological dependence because the user's brain feels enjoyment during the **rush** of a heroin high. The user's brain comes to associate this enjoyment with the heroin. This process works in other, non drug-related ways as well.

For example, someone might enjoy the taste of freshly-baked bread so much that the smell of another loaf prepares the brain to recreate the experience. Scientists are only now beginning to understand what happens during this process. They believe that heroin and such other drugs as alcohol release a substance called **dopamine** that rushes the pleasure message through part of the brain. In experiments conducted with rats, the test animals performed tasks to receive drugs that had triggered dopamine; when the rats' dopamine circuits were destroyed, the rats would no longer perform the tasks.

A user's psychological dependence is made stronger by the social part of using heroin. Heroin users almost always hang around with other people who are dependent on the drug. Even people who want to quit taking heroin find it difficult when every day they face social situations tied to drug use.

A heroin injector mixes the drugs with water in a teaspoon, heats it until it dissolves, and then draws it into the syringe.

The physical side

An important part of physical **dependence** to a drug is **tolerance,** or the way a user's body becomes used to a drug. Drug tolerance makes it necessary for the user to take more and more of the drug to reproduce the feeling of the first "high." It is this issue of tolerance that makes heroin so **addictive.** If a user has taken the drug regularly over a period of several weeks, he or she likely has had to take greater and greater amounts to achieve the same effect. When the drug has worn off, the user experiences drug cravings, restlessness, muscle and bone pain, stomach trouble, and other symptoms. At that point, the user is no longer driven by the perceived pleasure of the drug. Instead, he or she wants only to block out the pain that develops when the body begins crying out for another dose.

As the user develops tolerance and the need for increased amounts of heroin, he or she tends to progress through different methods of taking the drug. While snorting or smoking heroin provides a high for a beginning user, these methods are less effective at getting heroin into the bloodstream than **injecting.** Dependent users gradually move on to needles and **syringes.**

Other side effects

Regular use of heroin introduces a range of other health side effects. The greatest risk is contracting potentially deadly **hepatitis** or **HIV.** These illnesses are passed on in the exchange of bodily fluids. Infection can occur when people inject heroin with shared needles or syringes.

People dependent on heroin have little time for eating and sleeping properly. Therefore, they are often run down and vulnerable to other infections. Heroin also harms the digestive system, causing constipation and other stomach ailments. It also affects the **respiratory** system, leaving users prone to pneumonia and bronchitis.

ffOnce hooked you're never straight. You're either stoned, or you're ill. I'd say 60 percent of the time you're sick, 20 percent of the time you're racing around trying to get the stuff, and the last 20 percent you sleep.**JJ**

(Anonymous heroin addict, quoted in Andrew Tyler's *Street Drugs*)

Overdose and Withdrawal

To **overdose** on a drug means to take more of it than the body can tolerate. Heroin users risk overdose when a new supply of the drug has a greater **purity** than the normal supply. An overdose can happen within minutes, but it usually takes from one to twelve hours. When a person overdoses, the breathing becomes slow and irregular. Blood pressure drops, causing the skin to turn blue. Eventually, the user falls into a **coma**. Without treatment, the user can suffer from heart damage or **respiratory** failure and die. A person does not have to be dependent on heroin to overdose. Any heroin user who gets an unexpectedly large dose can suffer.

Withdrawal

Another well-known aspect of heroin **dependence** is **withdrawal.** A person who stops taking heroin after long, regular use becomes severely ill. The illness peaks about three days after the last heroin was taken. Symptoms of heroin withdrawal are similar to those of a particularly bad case of flu. They include fever, aching limbs, sweating, restlessness, cramps, and **insomnia.** The person's skin becomes terribly itchy and develops bumps resembling goose bumps, giving rise to the phrase "cold turkey." In addition, the user feels anxious and isolated and often has unsettling dreams.

Withdrawal symptoms fade after about a week or ten days, but the feeling of weakness and illnes can last for several months. By finally working through these last stages of withdrawal, the user overcomes most of the effects of physical dependence. However, even after successfully battling heroin withdrawal, many users return to the drug. Psychological dependence is a powerful factor in keeping heroin users hooked.

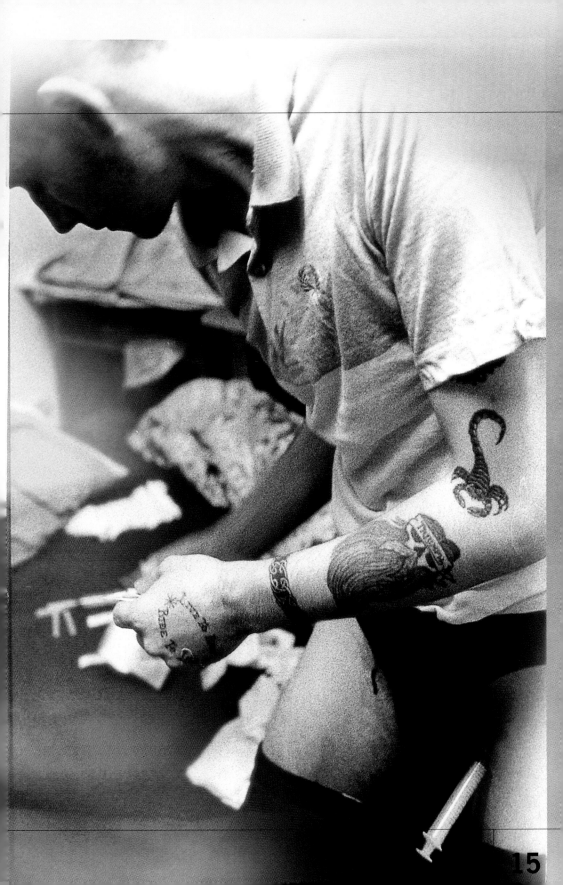

A Widespread Problem

Heroin abuse is growing at an alarming rate, according to drug officials. By the late 1990s, almost 600,000 Americans needed treatment for heroin addiction. By 1997, heroin use among students in grades 8, 10, and 12 had doubled or tripled, according to the National Institute on Drug Abuse. Unofficial estimates by drug counselors confirmed this overall rise in the use of heroin in that short period, and suggest that it has continued since then.

Increased supplies

While cocaine is still the most dominant illegal drug in many areas, the Colombian drug lords who helped make it so popular and available have used their well-established smuggling routes to branch into heroin production. The United Kingdom and Australia have also seen a rise in the amount of heroin being smuggled across the borders. These increased amounts of heroin were almost certainly linked to the rise in the number of **addicts.** As the drug became more available, its use spread, driving prices down. The **influx** of the drug has had other effects as well, and these effects make the heroin problem harder to attack. In the past, heroin was considered a drug of the inner city, where unemployment and poor social services drove people to use the drug. However, heroin use has now been documented across the United States. Rural areas have reported a sharp increase in heroin use throughout the 1990s. At the same time, a greater number of young people are being exposed to the drug.

Similar trends have been reported in Canada, Great Britain, Australia, and many other countries. There, too, wider availibility, greater **purity**, and lower prices have sparked an increase in heroin use. The drug is no longer confined to the more rundown neighborhoods of New York, Los Angeles, Toronto, or London. Increasingly, heroin is the drug of choice for many middle-class, suburban young people.

❝To see the comeback of heroin is scary. Once you're addicted to that, you'd sell your own kid for it.❞

(Robert Scanlon, director of the Bergen County (New Jersey) Prosecutor's Narcotics Task Force)

A Lengthy History

Although the form of heroin common today is only about 125 years old, **opiates** have played a part in human history for thousands of years. The opium poppy grows across central Asia, and there are records of the Assyrian and Babylonian civilizations using opium about 4,000 years ago. The Ancient Greeks and Romans also prized opium for its power to relax and calm people. The Greek goddess Demeter, for example, was said to use opium to soothe her sorrows. Morpheus, the Greek god of dreams and morphine's namesake, was often shown in artwork with a handful of opium poppies.

Arab traders introduced opiates to China between 600 and 900 A.D. Over the following centuries in China, **recreational** use of opiates grew. Far away in Europe, people during the Middle Ages began to use opiates for both medicinal purposes and pleasure. During the 1500s, Europeans saw a new form of opium called laudanum. The drug, named after a Latin word meaning "worthy of praise," was a mixture of heroin, alcohol, and spices.

The ancient Greeks associated their god of dreams, Morpheus (below), with opium poppies. Opium use became more widespread in the nineteenth century, when users would smoke it in secret dens (right).

Use and concern rises

By the mid-nineteenth century, use of laudanum and opium were increasingly common. Many English writers, including Thomas de Quincey, Samuel Taylor Coleridge, Charles Dickens, and Elizabeth Barrett Browning, claimed that the drug inspired them.

At that time, Chinese sailors started arriving at ports in Europe and the United States. They established "opium dens" where people could smoke the drug in secrecy. Many Chinese immigrants to the United States brought their drug habits with them, causing alarm.

By the early twentieth century, the United States had passed a series of laws against narcotics at the local, state, and national levels. Use of opium gradually decreased; however, punishment increased for selling the drug. By 1955, anyone convicted of providing heroin to anyone under eighteen was given the death penalty.

Modern refinements

The nineteenth century saw the changes that lead to the development of heroin. Morphine, the major active ingredient in heroin, was first purified in 1805. The hypodermic **syringe** was invented in 1853, making it possible to **inject** a liquid form of the drug. In 1874, German scientists modified the drug morphine to make it even stronger. This new form of morphine was called *heroisch*, which means *powerful* in German.

Heroisch was still different from today's heroin; the final version of the drug was produced in 1898. Scientists working for the Swiss chemical company Bayer altered morphine to make it more **soluble** in fat to enter the brain faster. This alteration produced heroin as we know it today.

Dealing with trouble

As soon at is was invented, heroin was hailed as a remarkable painkiller. It was supplied to hospitals and operating rooms. A form of heroin known as diamorphine is still given to thousands of cancer patients each year, as well as to women during childbirth. However, from the beginning, the powerful drug has also attracted non-medical users.

During the early part of the twentieth century, more and more people began taking heroin. Many became **addicted** to it. During the 1920s, controls on **opiate** trade were strengthened. Heroin was made illegal for non-medical uses in Europe and the United States. However, Great Britain did not ban the drug altogether. Its government set up a system in which **addicts** could have controlled amounts of heroin **prescribed** by a doctor.

Classical description of opium?

In about 700 B.C., Homer, the great poet of ancient Greece, wrote *The Odyssey*. In it he refers to a mysterious drug called "nepenthes," which "lulled all pain and gave forgetfulness of grief." Homer wrote, "No one that swallowed this dissolved in wine could shed a single tear that day, even for the death of his mother or father." Historians debate the identity of nepenthe. However, they agree that the effects described are almost identical to those of opium, a drug well known in Greece at that time.

Despite international attempts to curb the heroin trade, the opium poppy harvest remains a major money earner in many parts of the world.

The Modern Era

With its use banned in most countries, heroin became an **underground** drug from the 1920s onward. **Addicts** and casual users got their drugs through illegal sources. Secret laboratories produced heroin, and a complex network of **drug traffickers** kept most countries supplied with the drug.

The jazz saxophone player Charlie Parker (below) was one of many musicians whose lives were damaged by heroin use. The same problem arose among U.S. veterans after the Vietnam War a decade later.

The new wave

By the 1920s and 30s, heroin was widely viewed as a dangerous drug. The public had become aware of the risk of **dependence** and **overdose.** However, the 1960s was a different story. During that period, drug use increased in general. Many people who had tried so-called "softer" drugs like marijuana were curious about heroin. By then, young people had heard dire, and often exaggerated, warnings about drug use. They assumed that stories about heroin's addictive nature were also exaggerated. Many people who tried heroin at that time either found that they didn't like it or stopped after trying it once or twice. Unfortunately, many others got sucked into a pattern of dependence and self-perpetuating **addiction.**

Meanwhile, British heroin users got their supplies from a surprising source: the government. Some of the heroin sold on British streets during the 1960s had been obtained through an official system that allowed heroin to be **prescribed** by a doctor if a user could not face life without the drug. Some users managed to get ahold of surplus supplies of the drug and sold it to other users.

Trap for the poor

Today's pattern of heroin use dates back to the early 1970s. Like today, users were a mixture of the curious and the drug-dependent. Since then, the largest and most rapidly growing group of users has been people from **disadvantaged** backgrounds. During the 1970s, a variety of economic problems left many people without work or even hope of finding a job. In those situatioins and similar ones around the world today, heroin can become a way of coping with a dreary and seemingly hopeless life.

Who Takes Heroin?

Like other **derivatives** of opium, heroin's strength is its ability to block pain and produce a powerful sense of well-being. These qualities make it different from **stimulants** like amphetamines and cocaine, which seem to uplift users and make them more active or talkative. And unlike such **hallucinogenic** drugs as LSD, heroin does not create a kaleidoscope of intense sensations and emotions. Many heroin users describe the effects of the drug as being "wrapped in a cozy wool blanket."

A dead end?

For the most part, heroin is not the drug of choice for thrill seekers. Rather, people who are drawn to heroin often lead intolerable lives—they include the long-term unemployed, the poor, and other **disadvantaged** people. For them it offers a break from reality, a time when time itself doesn't matter. However, drug officials report that because heroin is so readily available and therefore fairly inexpensive, an increasing number of middle-class people are taking up the drug.

Heroin use, with its risks of **overdose,** poisoning, and **HIV** infection, is a problem in its own right. However, the growing number of heroin users indicates a wider social problem. Although high-profile heroin users like Kurt Cobain or Keith Richards grab headlines, most heroin users are young and seemingly ordinary. People who believe that only the most rundown inner-city neighborhoods have heroin problems are mistaken. By the late 1990s, the drug had reached middle-class suburbs as well.

Mixed signals

The use of heroin among the young has become a serious problem. Most surveys suggest an alarming increase in the number of young heroin users. Added to this, people are beginning to take the drug at a much earlier age than they did even ten years ago.

Part of the problem lies in recent media images of heroin use. The film *Trainspotting*, which was based on Irvine Welsh's hard-hitting novel about Scottish heroin users, opened in 1996. Although it graphically showed the negative side of the heroin scene, critics worried that the film also glamorized the use of the drug.

First, the main character, who should have looked like a haggard **junkie,** was played by a very healthy-looking Ewan McGregor. Second, the film was a worldwide hit, starting a fashion trend called *heroin chic*. Almost overnight, heroin **addiction** took on a high profile. Painfully thin fashion models posed in what looked like wrecked back streets. Heroin, once seen as a drug for losers, gained instant glamour.

A heroin user shows little interest in the outside world, retreating instead into a numbing cocoon.

A day in the life of a heroin user

For people dependent on heroin, the drug is a central point in their lives. Every day is characterized by the constant need to maintain a drug supply.

From the moment a heroin-**dependent** person wakes up, finding the next **fix** becomes the main concern. This means getting ahold of money, so the user may resort to petty crime such as burglary or shoplifting. Then he or she goes looking for a dealer, usually one who has had supplies in the past. For the dependent heroin user, life becomes a monotonous cycle of seeking and finding the drug fix. Sadly, many of the other people met during the day, including the dealer, are in the same position.

"After a while you need the drug to feel normal. Then you need more and more of the drug to keep feeling normal. Then you forget what normal is!"

(Heroin user and prison inmate)

Availability of Heroin

Nineteenth-century writers such as the poets Coleridge and Baudelaire viewed **opiates** as a spur to creativity. However, modern artists have provided different views of the heroin experience. The 1960s music group Velvet Underground recorded a powerful song called "Waiting for the Man." The song's title refered to a **junkie's** constant need for the drug and conjured up images of a heroin-**dependent** user's bleak life. The song, like the book *Junkie* by William Burroughs, captures the modern view of heroin as a depressing companion that drains the mind of any thoughts except the next fix.

A car radio seems like easy pickings for a heroin user desperate to get money for his next fix.

Heroin's black market

Because heroin is illegal except in the most exceptional circumstances, users must get supplies through the **black market.** The illegal trade in heroin is worth billions of dollars, but most of that money goes to the large-scale importers of the drug. At street level, heroin suppliers profit from sales, but very often the profit simply is used to feed the dealer's own drug habit.

Heavily dependent users rarely have ready cash of their own. They face the challenge of finding regular amounts to pay for each fix.

It is at this stage of dependence that heroin becomes closely linked to crime. Desperate users often resort to breaking into houses or cars and sometimes even robbing stores.

Police can usually recognize a drug-related robbery. Professional thieves usually have targets in mind before the robbery and therefore leave little evidence behind. In a drug-related robbery, however, property is usually ransacked as the drug user searches desperately for something that might be worth money if resold.

Firing blanks

For some people who have become dependent on heroin, the very act of **injecting** offers some form of comfort, even without heroin. A person with such a fixation will often fill a syringe with warm water and inject it into a vein. The injection, of course, has no real effect. But it reminds the user of the comfort that a heroin injection would supply.

Wider Effects

Heroin affects more than just the person who uses it regularly. The circumstances leading to heavy use can vary, as can the responses from user's family members and friends. However, the basic problem is the same: a heroin user's field of vision is narrowed so much by the drug that he or she cannot function without it.

Anger and confusion

It is quite common for the children of heroin-**dependent** parents to become dependent on the drug themselves. This is particularly true in areas worst hit by unemployment or poverty. The same lack of opportunity that turned the parents to heroin is still there twenty or thirty years later. Life becomes a depressing cycle in these circumstances, with no one able to see the problem with any sense of **perspective.**

It is a different story for families with no history of heroin involvement. Some parents deal with the problem by avoiding it, simply because it seems too hard to believe. They need advice, but they might be too ashamed to approach drug counselors or support groups. This lack of action, which essentially ignores the problem, creates a different kind of cycle. For both the user and his or her family, the only chance of stopping the cycle is facing the drug problem. However, for any solution to work, the user must be prepared to participate.

"Junk (heroin) is not like alcohol or weed (marijuana), a means to increased enjoyment of life. Junk is not a kick. It is a way of life."

(American novelist William Burroughs)

Price and Prevalence

One of the basic rules of **economics** is called the *Law of Supply and Demand.* Put simply, it means that the price of something rises or falls as a result of changes in how much is available (the supply) or how much people want to buy it (the demand). If supply increases faster than demand, then prices fall. If demand exceeds supply, then the prices go up.

The heroin trade shows this law at work. The demand for the drug is rising, but the supply is rising much faster. This causes the price to fall, which, in turn, makes it easier for new users to afford the drug. As a result, many countries are facing a dangerous problem of heroin abuse. One reason for the increase in heroin supplies is a recent period of good opium poppy harvests in Central and Eastern Asia, the traditional suppliers of heroin.

The heroin that actually reaches the street now is much purer than it was even ten years ago, so that current users face an extra risk of **overdose.**

Street prices

As a result of the extra supply, the price that heroin users pay for the drug has come down in real terms. The drug is usually sold in small packets of paper called *wraps,* which contain a small amount of heroin. A wrap might contain 50 milligrams of heroin, about enough for one hit for a new user, or perhaps 100 milligrams. The actual price averages about $25 for one-quarter of a gram, depending on the location.

The Heroin Industry

The heroin trade is a huge worldwide industry. In some ways it resembles other **commodities,** such as coffee and cocoa, because it reaches markets thousands of miles from its original source. Like coffee, the raw ingredient of heroin is grown, harvested, and **processed.** Like coffee, the first stage of heroin processing begins with the dry crop. For coffee, the process also involves roasting, grinding, and further processing. The process for heroin production is similar, with an additional chemical stage at the end. Morphine is extracted from the dried sap from the seed pods of opium poppies. Chemicals are added to the morphine to make it more **soluble** in fats. The result is heroin.

Medical uses

Heroin was developed as a tool for medicine, not as a **recreational** drug. During the late nineteenth century, doctors and **pharmaceutical** scientists had been searching for an effective painkiller for people who had undergone major surgery or had painful illnesses, such as cancer. The development of heroin in 1898 was hailed as a breakthrough in the medical world.

Heroin still occupies a place in medical science. Certain opiates provide effective pain relief for sufferers of **terminal** cancer and other conditions that lead to prolonged, uninterrupted pain. A close relative of heroin, called diamorphine, is sometimes given to relieve the pain of childbirth. These medical uses are all strictly controlled to prevent the spread of heroin to the **black market.**

A San Francisco drug clinic warns of the dangers associated with injecting heroin and other drugs.

> ➡ URGENT NOTICE ⬅
> There is a serious outbreak of Aids among S.F. Drug users! High Risk Haight Free Clinic ➡ Strongly Urges:
> DO NOT SHARE NEEDLES!

The Illegal Trade

It is illegal to trade in opium or in any related products, which include heroin. However, the demand for the drug is so great that the illegal heroin trade produces huge profits for those who are willing to risk getting caught. The heroin that reaches the streets of London or New York probably originated in a poppy field in Asia. Along the way, the price increases at each trading point. The last stop, the dealers, make some profit but often only enough to feed their own heroin habit.

Farmers and heroin

One of the biggest problems associated with the heroin trade is that opium poppies are an important source of income for poor Asian farmers. Getting them to turn to other crops is difficult, for several reasons. The governments in poppy-growing countries are often weak. They could not deal with the protests that would arise if farmers were forced to stop poppy **cultivation**. Substitute crops would not earn nearly as much money for these farmers.

Moreover, the regions in which poppies are grown are usually remote and difficult to monitor. In such places, opium poppy cultivation is part of the culture.

The illegal heroin trade begins in small villages in Southeast Asia, where many villages rely on income from supplying the drug.

Tackling the traffickers

Acknowledging the difficulty of keeping people from growing opium poppies, governments around the world have turned their attention to **drug trafficking.** It is during the middle stage of the heroin trade, when the drug is **processed** and sent around the world, that most of the illegal profits are made.

In 1988, several countries signed the United Nations Convention against Illegal Traffic in Narcotic Drugs and

Psychotropic Substances. This convention set guidelines for dealing with **money laundering**, the complicated method of turning drugs profits into legal money.

International agreements like the UN Convention also confront the issue of controlling the chemicals used to process opium and other plant-based substances into hard drugs such as heroin and cocaine.

From Asia to the United States

The whole issue of **drug trafficking** has had a huge effect on the United States. Asia remains the source of most heroin, but Mexico and Colombia have become major sources as well.

In Southeast Asia, warlords have turned an unsophisticated industry of hill tribes into a global heroin business. The wholesale product, which is sealed in plastic bags, costs about $170 in northern Burma. After relatively inexpensive processing and dilution, the same batch fetches up to $2 million in American and European cities.

This giant markup gets spread around. Horse or donkey caravans haul the drug from Burma to refineries in Laos and along the Thai-Burma border. Most of this refined heroin moves over jungle trails and mountains into Thailand, crossing the border far from government inspectors. The rest is smuggled to the United States through China and Hong Kong, or through India. Heroin comes to America hidden in various Asian exports, such as furniture or textiles. According to drug officials, 70 percent of the United States heroin supply enters the country through New Jersey.

The U.S. drug trade is largely controlled by organized crime. These criminals are sophisticated in the way that they import the drugs as well as the way that they hide their profits through **money laundering.**

Spanish customs police arrest a suspected drug trafficker in the port of Cadiz. Large amounts of heroin can be smuggled into countries on high-speed boats, which usually operate under the cover of darkness.

Legal Matters

The U.S. Drug Enforcement Agency (DEA) lists heroin among the most serious drugs of abuse in Schedule 1 of its drug classification. It is illegal to possess or supply heroin or related drugs to other people without a prescription. It is also illegal to produce, import, or export these drugs, or to allow premises to be used for their production or supply.

Heavier penalties

Anti-drug laws in most countries carry more severe penalties for trafficking than for possession of drugs for personal use. In the United States, for example, first-time offenders are sentenced up to five years in prison and are fined up to $2 million in fines. For repeat offenders, the penalty is up to 10 years in prison and a fine of up to $4 million. In many foreign countries, drug trafficking convictions can lead to a sentence of life imprisonment.

A police team smashes open the door of a suspected heroin dealer.

Controlled Substance Act

The Controlled Substances Act (CSA), Title II of the Comprehensive Drug Abuse Prevention and Control Act of 1970, is the legal foundation of the United States government's fight against the abuse of drugs and other substances. This law is a consolidation of many laws regulating the manufacture and distribution of narcotics, stimulants, depressants, hallucinogens, steroids, and chemicals used in the unlawful production of controlled substances.

Life with Heroin

A person who has become **dependent** on heroin gradually comes to think of only two things: how to get the drug and how to get it into the bloodstream fast. The fastest and most efficient way is by **injecting** it. In the distorted world of the dependent user, this experience is often compared to a near-death experience. As the drug is injected, the person sinks into a sense of **oblivion** that seems almost like dying. When the drug takes effect, the user feels a sense of joyful relief that they are alive again.

Dangers

Injecting, of course, introduces a number of serious risks for the heroin user. The most dangerous risk comes from using shared needles, which can lead to contracting **hepatitis** or the **HIV** virus. Sticking the needle into an artery—rather than a vein—is another. People have lost limbs as a result of such a mistake.

Arteries carry oxygen-rich blood to limbs and other parts of the body. If heroin is injected into an artery, it prevents oxygen from getting to its normal destination. Other problems are linked to mixing heroin with other drugs. Such combinations can produce vomiting and unconsciousness.

In addition, the repeated use of any drug leads to a strain on the liver.

Heroin use is especially dangerous for women. Because women have smaller livers than men, they have more severe side-effects. Heroin also stops ovulation and menstruation. If a heroin user becomes pregnant, she is likely to give birth to an underweight baby. There is also a higher risk that the baby will die within a week of birth. In addition, some babies born to heroin-dependent mothers show some signs of **withdrawal.**

Dozens of disgarded needles paint a dismal picture of the life of a regular heroin user.

Anything but nirvana

Sometimes, the rich and famous are drawn to heroin despite knowing the risks. Kurt Cobain, lead singer of the grunge band Nirvana, is one example. Cobain was born near Seattle in 1967. His childhood was unhappy, and it worsened when his parents divorced when he was nine. Cobain turned to "soft" drugs to cope with his depression. Things seemed to improve during the late 1980s when Kobain formed Nirvana. At first, Cobain was able to vent his **insecurities** and tension with songs like "Smells like Teen Spirit." The depression resurfaced, and Cobain looked for stability. He married fellow singer Courtney Love, but her influence was less than positive. The couple drifted in and out of heavy heroin use, risking losing their daughter. Cobain tried to stop taking heroin, but it had become the only source of comfort in an increasingly difficult life. The end came in April 1994, when Cobain went into his garage, took a great deal of heroin, and then shot himself with a shotgun.

An ex-user's story

Adam began dealing in marijuana when he was still at school. He viewed the experience as a big adventure, and enjoyed traveling abroad to get more supplies. The money he made enabled him to try other drugs, including LSD, cocaine, and heroin. Most of his friends believed that Adam was only a casual user of these drugs; unknown to them, Adam had become **dependent** on heroin.

Gradually, Adam realized that the heroin habit was taking hold of him; although he wanted to quit, he felt he couldn't. It was only after Adam took a large amount of cocaine to overcome a heavy dose of heroin that he changed his mind. The combination of the drugs caused Adam to pass out, and he didn't wake up for a full day. Adam finally acknowledged that the heroin use was causing him to risk his life. "When things like that started happening, I knew I had to do something," Adam said. In Adam's case, action was enrolling in Narcotics Anonymous to deal with his dependence. He was able to overcome his **dependence** and is now the father of three children.

45

Treatment and Counseling

There is no denying that it is difficult for an **addicted** heroin user to stop taking the drug. The process of **withdrawal** involves up to a week of physical discomfort. The flu-like symptoms are caused by the body's reaction to lack of heroin. Some users are able to go through this period on their own, driven by the need to get "clean." Others need the support of friends, family, or trained counselors to help them. They probably also need to learn to avoid situations that involve heroin use.

Uplifting pursuits such as yoga and meditation are helpful in allowing former heroin users to feel in control of their bodies.

Calling on others

Heroin users can turn to support groups to get help getting off the drug or to overcome their psychological dependence. Although there is no easy solution, many treatments use strategies developed for people with alcohol dependency. Organizations such as Narcotics Anonymous call for **abstinence** as a first step. This approach is backed up with meetings with other dependent users to build up a network of mutual help.

One type of treatment common in the United States is aimed at people who are still using heroin. It tries to find a way of replacing the heroin with methadone, another **opiate,** and lowering the doses in stages. Methadone treatment has a number of advantages. First, by offering a source of drugs, it reduces crime. Second, it can be taken orally, so that it carries no risk of infection with **HIV** or **hepatitis.**

Although some heroin users find themselves using methadone for years, they argue that it is their only hope of ridding themselves of dependence.

The Swiss strategy

In 1994, the Swiss government began a two-pronged program of dealing with heroin use. First, it aimed to reduce the risk of **overdose** and other health risks associated with **injecting.** Then it tried to tackle the problem of drug-related crime. The government actually imported 200 kilograms of heroin, which was then distributed under strict supervision to 1,146 Swiss **addicts**.

There was a small charge for each dose, but the heroin was free for those who could not afford it.

After three years, the program was declared a success by the World Health Organization. The levels of AIDS, hepatitis, and other blood disorders had dropped sharply, and the number of drug-related deaths was cut by half. While two-thirds of the addicts had been involved in crime at the beginning of the program, at the end that figure dropped to just three percent.

Treatment for addiction

In many drug treatment facilities, there has been increasing concern about heroin addiction. Many treatment centers address the issue of drug abuse using many approaches, including simply providing information and advice, helping people quit drugs, and supporting recovering drug users as they try to re-enter society. At most treatment facilities, the first appointment by drug users and their families is **confidential.** Such a meeting often includes sharing information and advice about treatment. Many facilities offer special services for young people that may include both home visits and support at the local juvenile court. Some drug users battling **dependency** are referred to special drug clinics for **detoxification** and to government agencies to help them find housing.

For people who have made the break from dependency, many treatment facilities provide follow-up support to help them stay off drugs. This support ties in with a range of local organizations, such as Narcotics Anonymous. Other programs provide ex-users with opportunities for education and employment.

Many clinics that provide methadone for registered addicts insist it is consumed on the premises.

Misgivings about methadone

Although methadone can effectively treat heroin addiction, it can generate problems of its own. It is even more **addictive** than heroin, produces longer **withdrawal** symptoms, and leads to more deaths from **overdose.** In addition, many users enhance the methadone high with other drugs.

People to Talk To

Over the years, the world has learned more about heroin and how it affects people. It has become clear that heroin is a drug that helps the user escape reality and can easily lead to a downward spiral of crime, illness, and even death.

Unfortunately, information about heroin is often distorted as it is passed on by word of mouth. Heroin using friends might even dare others to try the drug. This type of **peer pressure** is a strong and persuasive force.

Other voices

There are people who can put things in a different **perspective,** either by giving first-hand accounts of their own drug experiences or by outlining the clear dangers of heroin abuse. Parents and older family members are usually the best people to turn to. However, if you feel uncomfortable talking about drugs with your parents and teachers, there are many other ways to get information about heroin and other drugs.

The United States, like most countries, has a wide range of telephone sources where young people can find out more about heroin. Many of the organizations listed have confidential and toll-free phone lines. They provide information over the phone or can direct the caller to local agencies throughout the United States. Other groups are geared specifically to questions from younger people. When approaching one of these sources, the important thing is to be able to talk and listen openly and freely about your drug concerns.

Telephone helpline volunteers are able to provide confidential advice to people with heroin problems.

Information and Advice

The United States is well-served by organizations providing advice, counseling, and other information relating to drug use. The contacts listed on these pages are helpful sources for such advice or for providing confidential information over the telephone or by mail.

Drug awareness contacts

Center for Substance Abuse Prevention
5600 Fishers Lane, Rockwall II
Rockville, MD 20857
(310) 443-0365

Child Welfare League of America
440 First Street NW
Washington, DC 20001
(202) 638-2952
The Child Welfare League of America, based in Washington, provides useful contacts across the country in most topics relating to young people's problems, many of them related to drug involvement.

DARE America
P.O. Box 775
Dumfries, VA 22026
(703) 860-3273
Drug Abuse Resistance and Education (DARE) America is a national organization that links law-enforcement and educational resources to provide up-to-date and comprehensive information about all aspects of drug use.

Just Say No International
2000 Franklin St., Suite 400
Oakland, CA 94612
Call 1-800-258-2766 for the nearest youth group.

Narcotics Anonymous
P.O. Box 9999
Van Nuys, CA 91409
1-800-467-7314
Narcotics Anonymous (NA) is a network of self-help groups tackling the problem of drug dependence on the same lines as those of Alcoholics Anonymous.

National Institute on Drug Abuse
6001 Executive Blvd.
Bethesda, MD 20892
(301) 443-1124

Partnership for a Drug-free America
405 Lexington Avenue, 16th floor
New York, NY 10174
(212) 922-1560

Students Against Drugs and Alcohol
(SADA)
7443 E. 68th St.
Tulsa, OK 74133
(918) 249-1315

Youth Power
300 Lakeside Drive
Oakland, CA 94612
(510) 451-6666, Ext. 24
Youth Power is a nationwide organization involved in widening awareness of drug-related problems. It sponsors clubs and local affiliates across the country in an effort to help young people make their own sensible choices about drugs, and to work against the negative effects of peer pressure.

More Books to Read

Jaffe, Steven L., ed. Introduction by Barry R. McCaffrey. *Heroin*. Broomall, Pa.: Chelsea House Publishers, 1999.

Jaffe, Steven L., ed. Introduction by Barry R. McCaffrey. *How to Get Help*. Broomall, Pa.: Chelsea House Publishers, 1999.

Kuhn, Cynthia, Scott Swartzwelder, and Wilkie Wilson. *Buzzed*. New York, N.Y.: W.W. Norton and Company, 1998.

Littell, Mary Ann. *Heroin Drug Dangers*. Berkeley, N.J.: Enslow Publishers, Inc., 1999.

Mass, Wendy. *Teen Drug Abuse*. San Diego, Calif.: Lucent Books, 1997.

Pownall, Mark. *Heroin*. Austin, Tex.: Raintree Steck Vaughn Publishers, 1991.

Salak, John. *Drugs in Society: Are They Our Suicide Pill?* Brookfield, Conn.: Twenty-First Century Books, Inc., 1995.

Smith, Sandra L. *Heroin*. New York, N.Y.: The Rosen Publishing Group, Inc., 1993.

Woods, Geraldine. *Heroin*. Berkeley Heights, N.J.: Enslow Publishers, Inc., 1994.

Glossary

abstinence voluntary resistance, especially of an appetite or craving of a substance, such as a drug

addict person who is dependent on a drug

addicted condition of being dependent on a drug

addiction compulsive need for a habit-forming substance, such as a drug

addictive causing dependence or addiction

black market illegal trade of products such as drugs

coma state of prolonged unconsciousness caused by disease, injury, or poison

commodities products of agriculture or mining that are turned into products for sale

communist type of government in which property is owned by the community and the government greatly restricts personal liberty

confidential private or secret

cultivation growing and harvesting of crops

dependence/dependent physical or psychological craving for a habit-forming substance. A person dependent on alcohol cannot stop drinking.

derivative chemical substance related in form to another substance and capable of being obtained from it

detoxification process of removing poisons from the body

disadvantaged lacking in basic resources or conditions believed to be necessary for an equal position in society

dopamine chemical substance in the brain that regulates movement and emotion

drug traffickers/trafficking people who illegally transport drugs from one country to another are engaged in drug trafficking.

economics study of the production, distribution, and consumption of goods and services

epidemic large-scale outbreak of a disease or social problem

federal relating to the central government

fix slang term for a dose of heroin

hallucinogenic causing a person to hallucinate, or to see or hear imaginary things

hepatitis inflammation of the liver

HIV group of retroviruses that harm the immune system

influx sudden increase in supply

inject pump into the body, usually with a syringe

insecurities worries and anxieties that contribute to a lack of self-confidence

insomnia inability to sleep

instability quality of being unstable

junkie slang term for a drug addict or dealer

money laundering process of sending illegally obtained money through different bank accounts to make it appear to have come from legal sources

oblivion state of lacking active knowledge or consciousness

opiate any drug that contains or is **derived** from opium

overdose dose of a drug that is too much for the body to absorb and causes illness or death

peer pressure pressure from friends of the same age to behave in a certain way

perspective capacity to view things in their relative importance

pharmaceutical relating to the medical use of chemical sciences

prescribe give (by a doctor) a document requesting the supply of medicine

processed changed in some way to produce something for sale

psychotropic affecting mental activity and behavior

purity quality or state of being pure, or unmixed with another substance

recreational related to pleasure or entertainment

respiratory relating to the lungs or breathing

rush sudden surge of a drug's effects

soluble capable of being dissolved

stimulant type of drug that makes people feel more alert or energetic

syringe glass or plastic tube attached to a needle used to inject liquids into the body

terminal causing death

tolerance capacity of the body to accept or require more of a substance, such as a drug

tranquilizers drugs that induce calm or sleep

underground illegal and informal. Underground organizations act away from the view of the police or other law-enforcement groups.

withdrawal difficult process of giving up a habit-forming drug, and the negative physical effects this process creates

Index